SMOKiN' WEED WiTH JESUS

SMOKiN' WEED WiTH JESUS
The Gospel According to Cannabis

Clifford Beck

Smokin' Weed With Jesus
Cover Design Clifford Beck
Copyright©2015

"I always try to share with others the idea that in order to become compassionate it is not necessary to become religious."

-His Holiness the Fourteenth Dalai Lama

"Selfishness is not living your life as you wish. It is asking others to live their lives as you wish."

-Oscar Wilde

For My Brother, Randy

Chapter 1

The roads of Bridgeton were especially treacherous at night and with the outskirts of town poorly lit, anyone foolish enough to be traveling only invited disaster. It didn't have much to offer, save for a quiet life in a small town. An out-of-the-way tourist trap, Bridgeton was little more than a blip on the radar of Southern Maine, and with the soaking rains of spring, Route 302 could quickly become a driver's deathtrap, leaving one with the life-altering consequences of poor judgment and carelessness. For Richard, as though decided by fate or some rare alignment of the planets, the time of his undoing had arrived and would lead him down the path of what was soon to play out. In fact, it would be his own damn fault.

Richard was a bankruptcy attorney who had the unpleasant task of relieving businesses of their assets. Recently, he had taken an active role in parting the owner of a porn shop from his hard-earned money. Apparently, he had fallen behind on his taxes as a result of spending an inordinate amount on cocaine and prostitutes. Richard couldn't leave the property quickly enough, having felt soiled from the moment he walked in. But business was business. And business was good. The economy left many businesses, both large and small, on the ever-present edge of financial ruin. Richard always seemed to be there as the portent of corporate doom, representing a branch of law that people loved to hate, more so than others. Still, a job was a job.

    That night brought the usual spring rain as the sky grew heavy with a sullen, gunmetal gray. Richard was on his way home from the porn shop in Bridgeton. His briefcase contained the last of the paperwork on the adult retailer, soon to close its doors. All the i's were dotted, and all the t's were crossed. He had been doing the job for, at least, fifteen years, and as much as he tried to insulate himself from the emotional consequences of the financial trauma of others, he was never quite able to manage it. As a result, Richard had turned to alcohol to medicate his conscience. By the time his career reached its ten-year mark, he had become a consummate alcoholic, and the stress of his participation in a necessary evil was beginning to take its toll. His appearance had aged dramatically, beginning with hair loss and the need for bifocals. Later on, he developed diabetes, brought on by his consistent consumption of alcohol. But even this was not enough to extinguish his imminent self-destruction. Richard required an intervention, and it would soon be delivered to him personally.

    He was approaching Lake Sebago, the halfway point between Bridgeton and Portland. As usual, he kept a small cooler on the floor, behind the driver's seat. Like a pirate's chest, what it contained was, for Richard, of far more value than any hidden booty. In it was a fifth of three-year-old scotch. Just what the doctor ordered, as he passed the small beach to his right, he reached back toward the cooler and found it just beyond his grasp. Continuing to drive,

Richard turned back to locate the cooler, and having finally put a hand on it, turned to face the road. But before he could lay his eyes on the pavement, he was startled by the headlights of an oncoming truck. In his hasty search for his favorite stress reducer, Richard had inadvertently crossed the centerline. What happened next was unavoidable. There was simply not enough time to change course away from what was clearly the result of a bad decision, and the outcome would reach further than he could possibly imagine.

As death stared him in the face, every muscle in Richard's body stiffened while he tried desperately to recover. Time slowed to the pace of melting ice as he saw himself, as though from a distance, strike the front left corner of the truck. The force of the collision spun his car counterclockwise. But only a heartbeat later, the tires grabbed into the pavement, and the car's momentum sent it rolling down the road. Fifty feet later, it had come to a stop, landing hard on its roof. Richard, however, had been thrown from the car, coming to rest further down the road.

But, before his body came to a stop, Richard slid a few yards down the wet asphalt, shredding his clothes and grinding his skin down to bare flesh. However, on his way down the pavement, Richard had, again, become victimized by fate. In his path lay a small pothole, washed out from under the road. Its furthest edge grabbed him by the shoulder and ripped it away from its socket, tearing all its supporting tissue. The only structures to remain intact were nerves and blood vessels. If he survived, he would have, at least, a chance of keeping his arm -- if he survived.

By some miracle, Richard became conscious enough to open his eyes. He was remarkably free of pain but was unable to move. His mind was heavily obscured by the fog of trauma and shock. He was approached by quickly moving footsteps
    as he hung on the edge of unconsciousness.
    "Hey!" a voice yelled. "Can you hear me!?"

As his mind began to dim, Richard saw the man take out his phone. The next time he opened his eyes, he found himself staring up into the spinning rotors of a helicopter. As it left the ground, a flight nurse inserted an IV into his arm and hung a bag of fluids from a stainless steel bar welded into the ceiling. He felt the sting of the needle as his consciousness, again, drifted off.

The next stop for his broken body and displaced mind was the critical care unit of Maine Medical Center's emergency room. There, he would be assessed and stabilized by a team of trauma doctors and critical care nurses. Their goal would be to pull Richard away from the door of death and to help him recover as much of his life as possible. But they could only do so much, and eventually, the one thing Richard would need for a speedy recovery was the will to live. Even before his carelessness led him to slide down Route 302, the necessary part of himself that makes life worth living had been in short supply. Richard would have to recover much more than his shattered body.

Within thirty minutes, the life-flight helicopter touched down on the helipad of Portland's Maine Medical Center, where the trauma team waited nearby as the helicopter's rotors spun down to a stop. He had been placed on a backboard at the crash scene, and a cervical spine collar carefully applied around his neck. As the doors of the helicopter's medical bay opened, the doctors were able to get their first look at Richard's injuries. Those who had recently begun their trauma residencies were clearly disturbed by what they saw, while more seasoned doctors and nurses found their zone, blocking out any emotional reaction. This allowed them to think quickly and get the job done. The assessment of Richard's condition began as soon as the teams laid eyes on him.

His injuries initially led the doctors to assume that Richard was in grave condition. Upon impact with the road, Richards' head landed on its side, and as his body slid down the pavement, the rough asphalt grabbed his ear, ripping it away and down the side of his neck. Had his skull struck the road at a more acute angle, his brain would have quickly turned to the consistency of a bloody stew. But while the remains of his ear were recovered, this was not the most serious of his injuries. Richard had been thrown from a rolling car and skidded down the road like a pebble across a lake. His shoes had been pulled from his feet, his shirt torn from his body as his pants were forced down around his knees. Had he remained fully conscious, he would have certainly suffered the indignity of being helpless while in an almost complete state of undress. The skin on his chest, stomach, shoulders, and the side of his face had been ground off by the pavement, leaving his raw flesh exposed. In some places, his body had been burned down to its musculature, but it was his neck that gave doctors the most concern. On his way down 302, Richard had left the driver's window partly open, and not wearing his seatbelt only contributed to the potential for serious injury. As he was ejected from his car, his neck became nearly folded before his body's momentum shattered the window into a snowy storm of glass. But as quickly as the event had passed, his perception of time had slowed enough that he momentarily heard the crack of fracturing bone, leaving the underlying spinal tissue at risk of permanent damage. If he survived, he would be told the true severity of his injuries only upon his discharge from the hospital.

Accompanied by the flight nurse, the trauma team rolled Richard into the first bay of the critical care unit. They placed another IV, took X-rays, and began a more detailed examination. The x-rays confirmed the injuries suggested by his mangled body. But they also told of additional problems. His jaw had been both dislocated and badly broken, and many teeth on his right side had been shattered. Oddly enough, it had been his right hand that held the bottle of scotch, and although he had left it far behind, he received something to take its place. Pain. Unless he left the operating room in a shroud, Richard would be guaranteed a painful recovery. Hopefully, most of it would be masked by the gently consuming haze of drugs.

The CT showed no evidence of brain injury. In this respect, Richard was lucky. But the injuries to his jaw as well as his remaining teeth jumped off the computer display, and given the injury to his neck, Richard was rushed to surgery, so the fractured bones could be stabilized. With his brain intact, Richard's mind rose from the depths of unconsciousness. Now, unable to move his restrained neck, he was only able to look up at the fluorescent lights on the ceiling as he passed through the hallway leading away from the emergency room. They had identified him from the contents of his wallet, leaving a nurse to contact his family.

The trauma team took advantage of his wakefulness and proceeded to barrage him with questions. Did he know where he was? Could he move his fingers and toes? Could he follow commands? He was urged to remain as still as possible, but in spite of his willingness to follow instructions and the repeated assurances of the nurses, Richard was terrified. It wasn't so much dying he feared,

but being left disabled. It is truly amazing how a crisis can cause one to consider questions and ideas that had never before occurred to them. Perhaps it is when we are forced to face our mortality that we achieve the most growth. If this is true, then Richard was about to experience a great deal of growth. Once he arrived at the operating room, the trauma team handed him off to the surgical staff, who rolled him to the first suite available. While in critical care, his clothes had been cut off and any valuables turned over to security. Still semiconscious, Richard heard the tinkling of instruments being sorted as he was lifted over to the surgical table. He heard the doctor's voice as orders were given and the O.R. team organized into action.
"Hang a Diprovan drip, and let's get him under," the voice said.
There was a pause, and then Richard heard another voice.
"You mean, the Michael Jackson drug?"
For one brief moment, the room fell silent as all eyes became fixed on the O.R. nurse in charge. Then, one of the surgical technicians,

only moments later, was heard whispering the words,
"What the fuck?"
"Nurse," the doctor began. "Start the drip." His voice was firm and reflected a noticeable degree of agitation, as the nurse's face took on an expression of bewilderment.
"But I loved Michael Jackson," she whimpered.
She seemed to have become lost in her admiration for the deceased celebrity as she held the vial of white fluid loosely in her hand.
"Nurse!" the doctor repeated. "Hang the fucking drug or get out!"
Richard was terrified. At this point, he believed that if he didn't die of his injuries, the OR team would probably kill him out of sheer incompetence.
"But I did," the nurse continued.
She stood near Richards' head like a deer caught in a pair of headlights on a dark, wintry road, as the surgeon ordered that she be removed.
"Get her the fuck out of here!" he bellowed.

Two surgical technicians quickly approached her from each side, while an assistant relieved her of the vial of medication.

    The door of the surgical suite was opened, and she was dragged backward into the hallway. Halfway to the double doors, the nurse could be heard screaming.
"Why! Michael, why?! I loved you, Michael!" The surgeon collected himself and brought order to what had hovered on the edge of chaos as he ordered another nurse to administer the drip. Yet, down the hall, the nurse, who appeared to have gone somewhat insane, was being pulled through the double doors. However, there was a slight problem. They were dragging her through the doors faster than they would open, and her continued screams were suddenly blunted as the technicians, quite by accident, bashed the back of her skull against one of the heavy automatic doors. The resulting thud echoed through the hallway.
"Whoopsie," said one of the technicians.

The surgical team quietly chuckled amongst themselves as the procedure to repair Richard's broken body got underway.

As the nurse began the initial injection of the anesthetic, Richard was overtaken by an odd sensation. The drug had not yet entered his bloodstream when he felt himself drifting away. His faculties had completely cleared to the point of becoming hyper-aware. Taking a deep breath, he opened his eyes and found himself suspended near the ceiling of the surgical suite. One might think that a state of panic would quickly ensue, but Richard felt strangely calm, and looking down at his now anesthetized body, he was unable to recognize his own face. But, of all the feelings and thoughts one might have during a similar experience, Richard was overtaken by only one.
"Wow, this guy really fucked himself up." He continued watching from his ethereal vantage point as instruments were passed back and forth. He heard the sounds of an electric drill and the tapping of a stainless steel mallet. He watched as the play of life

and death unfolded below him when he suddenly felt himself being pulled through the ceiling. The event was free of even the slightest degree of discomfort as the world he knew fell away, replaced by a brilliant field of white. Richard experienced a warmth and peace that he could never have imagined. The light that surrounded him was blinding, yet he was not blinded by it. He simply drifted. There was no resistance, only warmth and peace. But somewhere in front of him was a small blue dot. It did occur to him that everything that had thus far transpired was simply the result of a heavily drugged mind yet, Richard possessed crystal clarity. But it was not only what he saw that seemed hyperreal, it was everything, as though his entire being had become ignited into a heightened state of awareness.

Chapter 2

He focused on the small, blue dot when it suddenly rushed towards him. Startled, Richard brought his hands up, shielding himself against something he could neither understand nor predict. As he opened his eyes, he felt a slightly warm breeze caress his face as a blue sky came into view. Looking down, he saw grass beneath his feet and a water fountain near his side. Out of curiosity, he reached down and, pushing on a chrome handle, took a cautious sip. It seemed to be just the right temperature, and Richard had never tasted anything like it. It was as though he was drinking water for the first time.

He wiped the water from his chin and, standing up, surveyed what appeared to be a city park, but it was oddly devoid of any of the typical sounds of an average city. Traffic, sirens, the milling about of people as they went on with the routine of daily life, and as Richard continued to scan his surroundings,

he couldn't help but notice that everyone within view was intently studying him. For a moment, Richard allowed his confusion to get the better of him as it quickly expressed itself in words.
"Where the fuck am I?"
Moments later, a child appeared in front of him. Richard looked down at her in surprise.
"Hey," he began. "What's your name?"
With blinding speed, the small girl moved closer to him and, drawing back a fist, punched him hard in the groin. The impact doubled him over as the child bellowed out a single demand.
"No swearing!" she yelled.
Richard paused as he tried to catch his breath.
"Okay," he gasped.
With his hands covering his aching testicles, he raised his head, only to find the child had vanished.

    Standing slowly, he noticed he was no longer being examined by those around him. Yet he felt that someone was still watching him. Off to his right, a man sat reclining on a park bench. He wore shoulder-length hair, a tie-dyed Grateful Dead T-shirt, and Bermuda shorts. And he was laughing. He motioned Richard towards him, and the closer he got, the more the man laughed.

"Gotcha right, and the stones, didn't she?" the man asked. "Come on, have a seat."

Still confused, Richard sat about three feet from him.

"So, Richard," the man continued. "Not doing so good, huh? Things a little fuzzy?"

Richard was further confused by the fact that the man, who, by all appearances, looked like a groupie, somehow knew his name.

"How did you know my name?" he asked. "And where am I?"

The man nodded his head.

"Those are good questions, but first things first."

Putting a hand in the pocket of his shorts, he pulled out a small butane lighter and something akin to a hand-rolled cigarette. He brought it up to his lips and, lighting it, inhaled deeply. Letting the smoke billow from his mouth, he handed it to Richard.

"Here, this'll take the edge off."

Holding it between his finger and thumb, Richard took an inquisitive smell of the smoke streaming from the burning end.

"Um, maybe not right now," he replied.

He passed it back to the man.

"All right," the man said. "More for me. Actually, there's a lot more where this came from."

He took another deep hit of what Richard now realized was marijuana.

"Well," he continued. "I imagine you've got a few questions, huh?"

After a moment's pause, Richard nodded and answered, "Yes, just a few."

"Okay," the man replied. "First, you're in heaven, okay?"

Richard took a breath in preparation for another question.

"Not yet," the man said. "We've got plenty of time. But tell me something: What's the last thing you remember?"

Richard thought hard about the man's question but could recall almost nothing.

"Um, I was driving," he said.

At that moment, he realized the seriousness of what had happened, as his expression quickly turned to shock.

"Am I dead?!" he asked. "And who are you?"

The man's tone became concerned as he answered what would be the first of many questions.

"Well, Richard," he began. "It's like this; I'm Jesus."

Richard's first thought was that he had been given some very powerful drugs after the accident. Or, maybe, he was drunk and passed out in his car, somewhere on the side of Route 302. But, because he strongly suspected the surroundings he found himself in couldn't possibly be real, Richard quickly rose from the bench and began pacing.

"None of this is right," he began. "You can't be Jesus!"

Jesus paused between hits of his joint.

"Why not?"

Bringing his hands up to his forehead, Richard continued pacing.

"Jesus wouldn't smoke weed! This has got to be some kinda' ...it's the drugs. They have to be giving me a lot of drugs."

"Richard," Jesus interrupted.
Richard continued ranting.
"Richard, calm down. Come here, have a seat."
Richard's near-psychotic stream of broken thoughts abruptly ended, replaced by the empty expression of dissociation.
"Come on, Richard," Jesus continued. "It's not that bad, is it? At least you won't have to close down any more porn shops."
Richard looked at him with a puzzled expression. "Now I remember. But how did 'you' know that? Were you watching?"
Jesus briefly chuckled at his question. "Watching you? No, I don't have time for that. I can see your whole life inside you. It's kinda like a psychic thing. Except that I'm Jesus."
Richard finally realized what had happened and jumped off the bench again, as Jesus rolled his eyes in frustration.
"I'm dead?" he yelled. "Shit! I'm fuckin' dead!"
Before Jesus could stop him in his tirade, the small girl who had chastised him earlier suddenly appeared in front of him. Seeing this, Jesus reacted in a low, quiet voice.

"Uh oh."

Again, the child rushed up to him faster than he could move and punched him squarely in the testicles. Richard reflexively cupped his genitals with both hands and dropped to his knees. The child was infuriated and pointed to Richard as she spoke. "Jesus!" she said.

Her voice was firm and reflected a heightened degree of agitation.

"This one has issues!"

Having taken a deep hit from his joint, Jesus exhaled the smoke upward, so as not to blow it in the child's face. After all, only grown-ups should be allowed to get high.

"I know," Jesus replied. "But he's new, so give him a break, okay?"

The child vanished as quickly as she had appeared as Jesus looked at Richard as though questioning his sanity.

"You're not very bright, are you? You'd think that you would have learned the first time, huh?"

Richard got back to his feet, but still bending over, continued to clutch his testicles as he groaned in pain.

"If I'm dead," he began. "Why does it hurt so much?" Jesus paused and nodded his head. "That's an easy one," he answered. "You still believe you're flesh and blood. You haven't let go yet, so when she punched you in the nads, you believed the pain was real. Dude, physically, you are someplace else."
After returning to the bench, Jesus again handed Richard the joint.
"You sure you don't want a hit?"
Richard looked at its smoldering tip.
"You know," he began. "I think I will."
He carefully took it between his finger and thumb and, bringing it to his lips, drew the smoke in and inhaled deeply. Jesus sat, looking on with a slight grin.
"So, what do you think?" he asked.
The effect was immediate and left Richard with a sense of clarity he had never before experienced, along with a noticeable euphoria. As he exhaled, he held the joint out, looking at it with an expression of surprise.
"Yeah, I know," Jesus began. "Pretty good, huh? I grow it myself."
Fascinated by its effects, Richard took another deep hit and felt something within him

awaken. He closed his eyes as he held in the smoke. But upon opening them, he became overwhelmed by the feeling that he had done so for the first time in his life.

"Wow," he said. "Too bad I couldn't get this stuff before."

He handed it back to Jesus, who, taking it, replied, "Nope, sorry. Enlightenment doesn't come cheap. You guys have to work for that."

As Jesus took the next hit, Richard craned his neck back and stared up at heaven's blue sky. Suddenly, the sky faded to black as an irregular, multicolored web filled the darkness.

"Here it comes," Jesus said.

Everyone in the park looked up and marveled at what they saw, as some could be heard expressing their wonder.

"Oh, ahh."

"What is that?" Richard asked.

"Take it in," Jesus answered. "It doesn't last very long."

Richard continued staring up at something he would never see again.

"But, what is it?"

Jesus paused to take another hit.

"You ready for this?" he asked. "That's your universe."

Still caught up in a profound state of wonder, Richard could only utter a single word.

"What?"

"Yeah, I know," Jesus replied. "I feel the same way every time I see it. Pretty awesome, isn't it?"

Moments later, the blue returned to the sky as the grandness of the universe faded away.

"That...was incredible," Richard said.

"Yeah," Jesus continued. "Hard to take it in all at once, isn't it?"

A moment went by as Jesus took another hit.

"So, where do we begin?"

"What do you mean?" Richard inquired.

"Well," Jesus replied. "You must have a few questions, and I have some things I need to talk to you about. Now, your name is Richard, right? So, that means your nickname is Dick."

Richard reacted with a bit of hesitation.

"Um, I really don't like that name," he said.

Jesus nodded his understanding.

"Well," he began. "Considering what you guys have become, I think it's appropriate. So, Dick, it is."
Richard saw no humor in this, and arguing was pointless. After all, no one tells Jesus what to do.
"Oh, come on, Dick," he continued. "It is funny, you know."
Richard spent a few moments stewing over his divinely bestowed nickname, but he suddenly became inquisitive about why he was being referred to as Dick.
"What do you mean 'what we've become'?"
Jesus took a last hit of his joint and crushing it between his fingertips, caused it to vanish.
Richard was mesmerized.
"How did you do that?"
"Dude, really?" Jesus said. "I'm Jesus, remember?"
Richard paused again.
"Oh, right," he said.
"Anyway," Jesus continued. "Everyone who comes here represents all of humankind."
Richard looked at him quizzically.

"Wait," he replied. "I have to answer for everyone. Really? Why? I'm not responsible for everyone else."
"Well, not personally," Jesus said. "But all of you have the same problem. It's you. You guys are your own worst enemy. Some of you cause your problems, and some of you just sit back and watch. Now, don't get me wrong here. I love all of you. But you suck. You have no idea how to treat each other. My boys wrote it all down, and you haven't listened to a word of it. So, yeah, all of you are equally responsible for the world you live in. Now, nobody wants to hear that. I get that..."
"But I can't do anything about that," Richard interrupted.
It seems that no one wants to be held responsible for the problems of the world.
"Dick," Jesus said.
He had this particular conversation with every new arrival. Whether they ended up staying was irrelevant. In the eyes of Jesus, everyone was held accountable.
"There's someone on your world. Who is it? Oh, the Dalai Lama. What a great guy. I really like him. Now, he said, 'If you don't

think one person can make a difference, you've never spent a night with a mosquito'. Man, I wish I could talk to him." Richard was stunned. The idea of individual responsibility had finally sunk in, but somehow he was having difficulty with the thought of the son of God sitting down for a one-on-one with the man believed to be the living Buddha.

"But he's a Buddhist, isn't he?" he replied.

Jesus shook his head in answer to Richards question.

"Wow," he began. "You 'are' quick, aren't you? But, really, what does it matter? All religions have one thing in common. They all teach peace. So, if you can live by that, then why would you need religion?"

Richard was puzzled. He found it hard to believe that Jesus would advocate for the dissolution of religion.

"But, aren't you, like, the founder of Christianity?"

Jesus had heard this time and again but maintained the patience typical of the Son of God.

"Me?" he answered. "No...I didn't create a religion. You guys did that. I was just the messenger."

Richard took a moment to process this response.

"Yeah, I get it," he said. "But what about the Ten Commandments?"

Jesus answered without hesitation.

"Well, first, that's part of the books of Moses. So, that's a Jewish thing. But, seriously, as long as you're doing the right thing and being nice to each other, you don't need any of that stuff."

Richard found this answer confusing and responded out of a need for clarity.

"So, let me get this straight," he began. "You're against religion?"

A moment went by as Jesus put considerable thought into his answer.

"Well, I didn't say that," he replied. "Some people need structure and support. But, a lot of people just need to get their heads out of their butts."

"Okay," Richard said. "I know a lot of those people."

"Yeah," Jesus said. "What do you call them conservatives? Dude, those guys are weird. Always thinking that 'their' religion is right and everyone else is gonna go to hell."
"Yeah," Richard said. "They kinda love to hate."
Jesus realized both the contradiction in terms and the logic of Richard's response.
"You know, Dick," he began. "That's a great way of putting it. They love to hate."
Jesus began to roll another joint as Richard closely surveyed his surroundings. No two trees were alike, and the grass was pristinely cut. There were elderly people sitting on park benches, and children playing in small groups. Richard motioned towards a small girl, sitting in the grass. Although she was alone, she still bore a broad smile.
"Where are her parents?" he asked.
Jesus took a deep hit of his joint. "They're not here yet," he replied.
Still watching the child, Richard posed his next question.
"So, she's alone?"
Now, Jesus also focused his attention on her.

"Nah," he began. "She's not alone. She knows they're coming. She can feel them. The sad thing is, she was never born. Some kind of accident. But she's here now, so it's all good."
From this answer, one word suddenly jumped out at Richard.
"Um, where exactly is 'here'?" he asked.
Jesus turned to him as he took another hit.
"Here is where you are," he began. "You must have heard this before: 'Wherever you go, there you are'. Right?"
Richard wasn't exactly a deep person and found this statement profoundly confusing.
"Uh...I don't get it," he answered.
"Okay," Jesus began.
Taking another hit from his joint, he took the time to formulate an understandable answer.
"It's like this; if you're standing way over there, where are you?"
"Um, over there," Richard replied.
Jesus sighed with frustration.
"Okay," he began. "Let's try something different."
Jesus snapped his fingers as both were transported to a place near the water fountain. Richard was startled to suddenly find himself

elsewhere, even though he was only yards away from the bench, where they had previously sat. Jesus put a hand on Richard's shoulder, trying to steady him.
"Take it easy, Dick. Don't go flippin' out on me."
Richard regained his bearings as Jesus prepared his next question.
"So," he continued. "Where are you now?"
Richard made a quick survey of his immediate surroundings and gave what, he thought, was a logical answer.
"We're at the water fountain."
Jesus took another hit from his joint.
"Yeah," he began. "But think about it on a different level."
Richard, again, expressed an obvious degree of confusion.
"Um...I still don't get it," he said.
The idea he was trying to convey to Richard would have to be illustrated by further demonstration, and snapping his fingers a second time brought them back to the park bench.
"Now, where are you?" Jesus asked. "Don't

think about what's nearby. That's all relative."
Pointing back to the water fountain, he asked, "You were over there before, right?"
Richard nodded but still seemed confused.
"Um, yeah," he answered.
"Okay," Jesus continued. "So you were there and now you're..."
A few moments went by as Richard processed the question put before him.
"You're here, right?" Jesus asked.
Richard's eyes widened with the feeling of an approaching epiphany. Jesus snapped his fingers again, sending them back to the water fountain. "Now, where are you?"
The idea was almost too much for Richard to process. Many times, the most basic concepts become grossly overthought by our need to bring order through complexity. Hundreds of books have been written about one idea because we believe that to be deserving of human understanding, the simplest of things must be made complex. We must remake them, not as tools of enlightenment, but as issues to be discussed and dissected over centuries by philosophers and scores of

religious leaders. The answer came to Richard in a flash.
"I'm here."
Jesus smiled and nodded. Snapping his fingers again brought them back to the bench.
"Now, where are you?" he asked.
Richard was struck with something he had never experienced, and although it was fleeting, I
was, nonetheless, something that induced a change in how he perceived himself.
"I'm here," he said.
He realized that being 'here' was not a matter of where he was. 'Here' is not a place but a moment of completeness, something that lies beyond the objective, defining the core of one's being. Richard took a gasp as the pieces fell together.
"I'm here," he began. "I'm always here. Wherever I am, I'm here!"
Jesus smiled broadly as he handed him his joint.
"I think you got it," he said. "Now, if everyone on your world could understand that."

Richard brought the joint to his lips and took another hit as, once again, the universe opened over his head. Exhaling the smoke, he marveled at the celestial architecture of existence. The birthplace of all things. Richard spent a moment staring at the joint. "What is this stuff?" he asked.

"I don't think you're asking the right question," Jesus replied. "I think what you really want to know is how it is that you can look up and see that, right? Okay, here's the thing. You guys have never been able to see past what you call 'reality'. I'm not saying you should be able to do that. You definitely would not be able to handle it. The problem is that you never dig any deeper than the surface."

Richard was confused as to the direction the conversation was taking, which revealed itself in his expression.

"Okay," Jesus continued. "Here's a good example. You guys like to judge each other. A lot. You don't take the time to sit down and get to know someone. You just draw your opinions, and that's it. Right?"

Now, Richard realized that it wasn't about being able to see the universe. The point of the conversation was how people treat each other.

"Here's another good example," Jesus continued. "You got something called the Bible, right? But no one reads it. Oh, yeah, you read the words, but just because it says it's the word of God doesn't mean you take it literally. I mean, that's not very bright, is it?"

"You know," Richard replied. "I don't really read it much."

Jesus nodded while taking another hit of his joint.

"Dick," he began. "You're probably better off." Richard was shocked. Standing in front of him was the son of God, who seemed to be advocating the abandonment of the Bible.

"So, people should stop reading the Bible?" he asked.

Jesus exhaled the smoke as his eyes visibly dilated. "Well," he continued. "Most of it you don't really need. The Jews only study the first five books of the Old Testament, and people who call themselves 'Christians' have the Gospels. Why would you need anything else? And why would you need religion anyway? Religion's just a bunch of rules. The only thing you need is spirituality. You just do the right thing and be nice to each other, and you've got it covered"

Richard focused on every word.

"I never really thought about that," he said.

"Yeah, I know," Jesus replied. "None of you do. You're all so caught up in yourselves that you throw out what you're not comfortable with and judge people with the rest. That's not what it's all about, Dick. Now, don't get me wrong. It doesn't matter to me what religion you follow. If you want to be a Buddhist, be a Buddhist. If you want to be a Jew, be a Jew. It doesn't matter. They all teach the same foundation anyway. So, it's not about religion, and actually, religion has its limits. You can't grow spiritually by following a bunch of rules. It just doesn't work that way."

He then pointed out that the Dalai Lama once said that religion was unnecessary as long as one follows the practice of compassion, kindness, and giving. He went on to say that these ideas are common to all religions as well as other belief systems, rendering religion obsolete.

"And speaking of compassion," Jesus continued. "You guys have a problem with being touched, don't you? Tell me something. You can beat the crap out of each other with your bare hands, but you bump into someone in a store, and you apologize for touching them. How does that work?"

It wasn't that Jesus was right; it was how to make sense of something that was, in itself, ridiculous, yet part of human nature. Richard's struggle for an answer proved fruitless.

"We're pretty hopeless, aren't we?" he replied.

"Hopeless? No," Jesus answered.

"Misguided? Absolutely."

Jesus continued by telling him that simple human touch conveys many things that exist beyond language. Emotions, compassion, and comforting, to name a few. However, labels are not enough to provide the experience of touch with any objective definition. Jesus further pointed out that human beings have always found it far easier to make physical contact through violence than through warmth and compassion. Jesus rolled another joint and, lighting it took a deep hit. Richard, having noticed how much weed Jesus smokes, inquired about his frequent use.

"So, if you're Jesus, shouldn't you already be enlightened without smoking that?"

Jesus raised his head and blew out a heavy column of smoke.

"You know," he replied. "I never thought about that."

Without so much as further considering Richard's question, he brought the joint back up to his lips for another hit.

"Oh, I just thought of something," he said. "It used to be that when someone was dying, you'd let them go. Not that you had a choice, but you said your goodbyes and stayed with them, right up until the end and then found a way to move on. Now, you put people on machines, and you give them drugs to keep them alive, no matter what. I mean, don't you think it's a little cruel to make people suffer like that?"

Richard agreed wholeheartedly and explained that the prolonging of one's life is generally decided by their family. Doctors only provide information.

"Is that it?" Jesus asked. "Let me guess, it all comes down to legal stuff, doesn't it? Right and wrong, just go out the window."
"Um, yeah," Richard replied.
He found this a particularly uncomfortable moment. Even in the practice of bankruptcy law, he knew that matters of life and death were especially complicated. Far more than necessary. Having already spoken of a much-needed step in spiritual evolution, Jesus reiterated this point, saying that it is not so much faith in an afterlife that's important but what is best for the person whose life has been reduced to a mechanical existence. Faith comes later, sometimes appearing on the doorstep of one's demise. Breaking away from the seriousness of the conversation, Richard asked what he thought was probably a stupid question.
"So," he began. "Is Buddha here somewhere?"
Jesus looked at him with surprise.
"Buddha?" he replied. "Nice guy, definitely one of my favorite people, but he taught the idea of nonexistence, so I don't know where he is."

There was a pause in the conversation as Richard tried to think of more questions. After all, how often does one get to talk to Jesus?

"What about Muslims? Are they here?"

Jesus hemmed and hawed at Richard's question, but finally gave an answer.

"You know," he said. "We had to kinda split the property if you know what I mean. But that's a really long story."

He raised a hand and pointed off into the distance. "Now, if you go that way, keep going until you hit sand, and they'll be right there."

"Really?" Richard asked.

He was struck with surprise at the idea that Muslims could, even partly, occupy an ethereal territory with the Christian Messiah.

"Yeah, why not?" Jesus answered. "Everyone's pretty much the same anyway, and God doesn't have a religion. So, why not?"

Richard sat on the bench in silence as he absorbed the conversation.

"There is another question you want to ask, isn't there?" Jesus said.

Richard's thoughts drifted away, but his attention suddenly snapped back to the sound of Jesus's voice. "What?" he asked.
With his joint having gone out, Jesus relit it and smiled patiently.
"Come on, Dick," he began. "You know. The question. The one that everyone asks. They get here, and they all ask that one question. You know what I mean."
Richard paused to think, but he honestly didn't know what Jesus was talking about.
"Really?" Jesus asked.
He was truly dismayed by Richard's confusion and found his lost expression somewhat humorous.
"Are you serious? You don't know what question I'm talking about?"
Jesus stretched out his hands and tipped his face up to the heavenly sky.
"Dude, it's the question," he continued. "The big question. The one everyone's trying to answer."
It took a few moments, but the question Jesus was referring to eventually dawned on him.
"Oh, right," Richard said. "You mean the meaning of life?"

Jesus let out a heavy sigh of relief.
"Wow!" he began. "You seriously had me worried for a moment."
Jesus waited briefly for Richard to ask the question.
"So," he continued. "Go ahead, ask me."
"Um... I thought you were just going to tell me," Richard said.
Jesus took another hit from his joint and shook his head slightly.
"Dick, seriously?" he said. "How do you expect to learn anything about life without putting in some effort? I can't do everything for you. You have to do some reflecting. Ask the hard questions and deal with the answers, even if you don't like the answers you get. But you have to be the one to ask."
"Um, alright," Richard began. "What's the meaning of life?"
Jesus smiled broadly as he flicked some ash from the end of his joint.
"I thought you'd never ask."
He took a moment to gather his thoughts as he smoked the last of his joint.
"Okay," he continued. "Where do we start?"
Another pause went by.

"Life has no meaning. It's just something that happens. But here's the thing: you guys think that life should have meaning because asking the question makes you feel like you're here on purpose. So, your existence has to have some kind of meaning. So, I'll make it easy for you. I won't give you all the details because they're not important. But check this out: instead of looking for the meaning of life, look for the meaning of 'your' life. Now, that's a lot harder, isn't it?"
Richard was clearly confused. There had been many books and articles written about the meaning of life, but not the meaning of living.
"You see," Jesus continued. "Anyone can die, but not everyone can live."
Richard was still confused. Not by what the question had become, but by the fact that the answer must be approached by the individual alone. Seeing the expression on Richard's face, Jesus saw the need to interrupt his train of thought, snapping his fingers several times in front of his face.
"Dick," he said. "Earth to Dick."

His concentration having been broken, Richard's attention was immediately directed back to Jesus.

"Sorry," he began. "I was just thinking."

Jesus nodded as he took out a small ceramic pipe, filled the bowl, and lighting it, took a deep hit.

"Yeah, I get it," he began. "But here's another thing. It's not a deep question and if you start thinking about it, you're never going to get an answer. It's uh...a Buddhist kind of thing. Some of the most important questions can't be answered with logic. Get it?"

Richard paused to let the words sink in, but this time, he allowed his sense of logic to momentarily slip. The answer, then, made itself clear.

"So, it's all about living proactively, right?"

Jesus nodded with a broad smile as he passed his pipe to him.

"Now you're getting it," he answered.

"But how you do that is up to you. So, you can't go around telling people how to live their lives when they're trying to reach their own goals."

After taking a deep, long hit, Richard passed the pipe back to Jesus. But, he was struck by a curious question.

"I don't mean to get off track, but where do you get this?"

Jesus looked at him with a grin.

"You really wanna know?" he asked. "Here, stand up."

Both got to their feet while Richard considered the odd nature of Jesus's request.

"You ready?" Jesus asked.

"Yeah, I guess," Richard replied.

"Okay," Jesus continued. "Strap in."

Jesus snapped his fingers, instantly transporting them to a vast field of marijuana. Under the royal blue sky of heaven, the tall waving plants seemed to go on forever. Their buds grew like clusters of grapes and gave off a golden glow. Richard quickly became hypnotized by the aroma wafting on the breeze.

"It smells like honey," he said.

"Yeah," Jesus began. "Grew it myself. I call it 'toasted honey'. Get it? Toasted?"

Richard was stunned. He didn't know much about Christianity or the Bible, but he never

imagined the son of God to be so laid back, much less a connoisseur and cultivator of a type of marijuana that induced instant enlightenment.
"So, you smoke it 'and' you grow it. Not exactly what I would have imagined," he said.
Having heard this remark from others, Jesus already had a humorous response.
"Come on, Dick," he began. "Give me a break. Now, who's going to have the best weed in the universe? Me. 'Cause I'm Jesus, right?"
The question did not require an answer. After all, who in their right mind would argue with the son of God?
Jesus again snapped his fingers, transporting them back to the park bench.
"Have a seat, Dick," Jesus said.
They both sat as Richard, once more, studied his surroundings. It all looked so peaceful, but Richard was struck by the feeling that what he was seeing wasn't real. Perhaps the person he had been speaking to all this time was a fiction, the product of a drug-saturated mind.
"So," he began. "This is heaven, huh?"
Jesus paused in his response.

"Well, yes and no. Kind of," he answered. "This is heaven for you."

Richard tried to process his answer. It wasn't enough that his body lay under anesthesia, somewhere on the line between life and death. Now, he had to figure out the nature of divine reality. He shook his head in confusion.

"I don't get it," he said.

"That's okay, Dick," Jesus replied. "We've got plenty of time."

He turned toward Richard and put an arm across the top of the bench.

"Okay, it's like this," he began. "It's all a matter of what you're used to. Look around. Does any of this seem familiar to you?"

Richard surveyed the park again, taking note of where the benches were. The trees. The water fountain behind them.

"Yeah," he answered. "This is Deering Oaks! But, where are all the buildings? Where's the post office?"

Jesus already had an answer.

"Well, you don't like the city very much, do you?" Richard's response was immediate.

"Actually, I can't stand the city, but I've always liked this park."

Jesus emptied the bowl of his pipe while nodding his head.

"You're almost there," he said. "Now remember, don't think about it too hard."

As much as Richard thought about it, he was unable to realize the true nature of his surroundings.

"Um, I'm not really getting it," he said.

Jesus slipped the pipe into a pocket of his Bermuda shorts.

"Wait, no more weed?" Richard asked.

"Nah," he answered. "To be honest, I'm getting kinda hungry. Hey, how about a pizza? Maybe a couple of beers?"

Jesus seemed to be full of surprises, and Richard was astonished at the idea of the Son of God sitting down for pizza and beer.

"Beer?" he asked. "Really?"

Jesus rolled his eyes as if Richard should know better than to ask.

"Dude, seriously?" he asked. "I turned water into wine once, remember? So, I think it's okay that I have a cold one once in a while. So how about that pizza?"

Richard was not at all hungry. In fact, it hadn't occurred to him that even on death's

door, he could eat at all. He was still trying to process everything that had happened.
"Um, maybe later," he answered.
"Okay," Jesus replied. "So, anyway. Let's say that instead of ending up here, you landed someplace that looked like, I don't know, northern China. How would you handle that?"
It took only a few moments for Richard to answer.
"That would be kinda weird," he said.
"Okay, why?" Jesus asked.
"Well," Richard answered. "I've never been to northern China."
"Okay," Jesus replied. "So basically, you'd be lost, right?"
"Well, yeah," Richard answered.
Jesus let a moment pass, allowing Richard to reach the natural conclusion of the question at hand. What is the nature of heaven?
"Dick," Jesus said. "It's the same thing here. You show up to whatever you were drawn to back in your earthly life. Otherwise, you'd be lost. Your existence would be chaotic."
Now it made sense. Heaven is, at least in part, a state of the soul. The places and probably the people one is drawn to in life become part

of one's being and act as a reference point for one's ethereal existence. Richard experienced a moment of profound illumination as he realized the answer to a question that had been pondered over centuries, but this was followed by another question.

"What about hell?" Richard asked.

If heaven has its basis in earthly life, what is hell based on? Some religious and literary sources describe it as a place of eternal suffering. The

Greeks conceived of hell as a place named Tartarus, where the most wretched of souls were cast into an abyss of blackness, tortured for their evil deeds until the end of time.

"Hell," Jesus began. "It's kinda the same thing. It's a state of the soul, but if you lived life to hurt people and make them miserable, then that's what you're going to end up with."

Richard listened intently as Jesus described what philosophers and theologians had been discussing for hundreds of years.

"It all comes down to this," he continued. "In the end, you get what you give. If you bring joy to people, that's what you get. If you cause misery and pain, then you get that. Pretty simple, huh?"

The answer was crystal clear, but there was one remaining question. Who makes the decision?

Who is responsible for sifting through humanity, sorting out the good from the evil? When asked, the response Jesus gave was not what Richard expected. "I don't send people to hell," Jesus answered.

"That's not really in the job description. But everyone makes a choice. You can be a good person, or you can be a dick. Don't get me wrong. No one's perfect. People make mistakes, and that's fine. And sometimes people get hurt by those mistakes. But to decide to live that kind of life is very different. So, when you kick off, you get back all the pain you caused. That's just the way it is."

Having put the pieces together, Richard now saw the bigger picture.

"So," he began. "We send ourselves to hell, right?"

"Pretty much," Jesus replied. "You have the right to make your own decisions, but you have the responsibility to deal with the consequences, and there's nothing I can do about that."

"So, I guess you can't fix our problems, can you?" Richard asked.

The earthly world had been irreparably damaged, and humanity was dangerously teetering on the edge of self-destruction.

"Like I said," Jesus answered. "There's nothing I can do."

Richard was puzzled. Certainly, the Son of God was capable of undoing everything that mankind had caused and bring them back from the edge of extinction. Sensing Richard's bewilderment, Jesus offered a clearer explanation.

"Think about it this way," he continued. "You treat the planet you live on like rock stars in a four-star hotel room. When you walk in for the first time, it's beautiful. It's a work of art. But when you leave, it's trashed, and the manager is not happy. And worst of all, you don't seem to care. Some of you do. But it's never going to be enough, and if the big guy stepped in, everything would turn to chaos. The difference between your reality and divine reality would leave all of you guys sitting in a puddle of your own poo, drooling on the floor. You just wouldn't be able to resolve it."

Hearing this, Richard resigned himself to the understanding that human survival is a hopeless endeavor and has likely always been. "So, is that it?" he asked. "Are we that hopeless?"
"I didn't say you were hopeless," Jesus answered. "You just don't care. There's a huge difference. If you want a future, you have to get rid of your apathy and start working for it."
Richard sat in disappointment. Surely, if anyone could intervene for the sake of preventing humanity's self-destruction, it would be the Son of God. Without divine involvement, Richard realized that the human world was truly fucked. Seeing his expression, Jesus gave him a gentle shove at the shoulder.
"Come on, Dick," Jesus began. "Cheer up, it's not all that bad."
Richard turned to him with a puzzled look.

"It's not all that bad," he said. "How could things possibly be any worse?"

"Well," Jesus replied. "At least your mouth isn't next to your butthole. Imagine taking a dump when you're getting your teeth cleaned. Now, how much worse would that be?"

Richard supposed this was true, despite how ridiculous the idea was. But it did nothing for his realization that his world was likely beyond recovery.

"You know," Richard began. "Maybe I will have that pizza."

Jesus nodded in approval.

"Excellent!" he said. "You wanna beer?"

Richard was still bewildered by the idea of smoking weed with Jesus. But it 'was' heaven, so why the hell not?

"Uh, yeah, sure," Richard answered.

It was only a few moments later that a small light appeared in the sky, and as it drifted closer, it grew brighter. But the object was silent and prompted Richard into a palpable degree of fear. Jesus eagerly rubbed his hands together.

"Ah, our pizza's here," he said.

He glanced over at Richard, noticing his tense expression, and, reaching out his hand, tapped him on the shoulder.
"You're really going to like this."
The illuminated object gently touched down in front of them, and as the light faded, Richard was stunned to see an angel standing before them. To say its appearance was grandiose would be a vast understatement. It was a thing of beauty beyond words. Its wings shimmered a pale blue. Its hair, long and white appeared perfectly coiffed and radiant.
"Gabriel!" Jesus said. "What's shakin' my man?"
They greeted each other with a fist bump.
"Same old thing," Gabriel replied. "Just delivering the best pizza ever!"
Richard was overtaken by a feeling of surprise that bordered on shock. Just when he felt that his experience couldn't be any more surreal, he found the Archangel Gabriel delivering pizza and beer. As Gabriel's wings folded onto his back, Richard noticed something that truly tried his sanity. Gabriel was wearing a white baseball cap that displayed the words 'Pizza Heaven' in bold

black letters. Richard was shaken back into the moment as Gabriel continued.

"So, this is him, huh?" he said. "Dick, right?" Handing them each a bottle of cold beer, Gabriel briefly inquired about Richard's presence.

"So, are we keeping this one or are you gonna throw him back?"

Jesus turned to Richard with an expression of uncertainty.

"Mmm," he began. "I don't know yet, but we'll get to that later."

Having delivered the pizza and beer, Gabriel stood back and opened his wings. Again, Richard was awestruck by the sight of such magnificence.

"Well," Gabriel began. "Gotta fly."

"Hey, hang on!" Jesus interrupted. "Don't you want a tip?"

Richard looked on in amazement as Jesus gave him a joint.

"Here ya' go. Enjoy."

Taking the joint. Gabriel brought it to his nose and deeply took in its aroma.

"Ah, you're the best," he said.

"Hey, my weed is your weed," Jesus replied.

Gabriel brought it to his lips as Jesus reached up and lit it.

"Allow me," he said.

Taking a deep hit, Gabriel experienced its effects immediately, as he saw within himself his own birth. A wafting ethereal feather, born from the singular light of God. The seed of his soul. The essence of his angelic being. Tipping back his head, he blew a heavy column of smoke toward the sky, gave Richard a wink, and vanished. Again, Richard's expression fell into one of disbelief.

"What?" Jesus asked.

"Uh...nothing," Richard replied.

Jesus laid the pizza box on the bench. Inside was something that could only come from the heart and soul of paradise. A pizza like no other. One that put all others to shame. The box was opened, revealing to Richard a true work of art. Like some great noble truth, it lay in front of him. Its crust perfectly browned, with cheese glowing an ethereal golden color. And the smell. It struck Richard's senses with the force of a freight train. A freight train of steaming, cheesy goodness. Jesus handed him the first slice.

"Here," he began. "Check this out."
The smell grew more powerful as he brought the slice to his lips, and for a brief moment, Richard became slightly delirious.

But that soon passed as he took his first bite. The experience was far more heavenly than heaven itself, and Richard quickly concluded that the pizza, delivered by the Archangel Gabriel at the request of the son of God, beneath the blue sky of heaven, was the most wonderful thing he'd ever stuck in his mouth. But this soul-elevating experience was interrupted as Jesus spoke in a jesting manner.
"You know, the cheese is made from angel puke."
Richard suddenly broke out into a coughing fit as Jesus reached over and gave him a firm slap on the back.
"Are you serious?" he gasped.
Jesus grinned as he gave Richard's shoulder a friendly squeeze.
"Dude, I'm just messing with you," he said.
Yet again, Richard's face took on an expression of confusion.
"What?" he asked.

Thus far, Jesus seemed to be the jovial sort, but a sense of humor wasn't what Richard expected from the son of God.
"What, I can't have a sense of humor 'cause I'm Jesus? Really?"
They continued with their meal while Jesus spoke between bites of pizza and sips of beer.
"Oh, how's the beer, by the way?"
Richard had already drunk half the bottle. And yes, Jesus took notice.
"Wow, that was quick," he said. "I'm guessing that's how you wrecked your car, huh?"
Richard should not have been surprised to realize that Jesus knew of his accident. Yet his expression revealed exactly that.
"Um, were you there?" he asked.
Jesus chuckled briefly at his expense.
"Don't be ridiculous," he said. "And you still don't get it, do you? Look, if you think that me and the big guy are always gonna be there to pull your butt out of the fire, then don't hold your breath. We're not your babysitters. You're all supposed to be big boys and girls by now, and when you make mistakes, you are the ones who have to deal with them. How are you supposed to learn how to live your

lives if we step in and clean up your messes for you? You guys have got to learn to change your own diapers."

There was a pause as each took another slice of pizza.

"Let's talk about something else," Jesus said. There was one issue he felt was necessary to bring up and critical to the welfare of humankind. In fact, he saw it as having the same degree of importance as spirituality.

"I'm just gonna lay it out for you," Jesus began. "You guys have a serious problem." Richard's attention was immediately focused on the seriousness of his voice. He thought Jesus might be referring to guns, politics, or the rampant spread of human stupidity.

"Well, we have a lot of problems," he began. "Which one are you talking about?"

It's the one problem that's caused all the others," Jesus replied.

Richard paused to consider what he saw as a vague hint.

"It could be anything," he thought.

What is the one thing responsible for turning the human species into something truly fucked up? Richard entertained several possibilities: money, poverty, war, and hunger. Perhaps, somewhere along the evolutionary past, someone or something simply stepped up and took a giant piss in the human gene pool. But, Richard had the feeling that it was something so basic that it lay beyond any degree of consideration. Yes, it was something that hid in plain sight like a snake preparing to make its way up the leg of a child's pants.

"Don't think about it too hard now," Jesus said.

A few more moments went by as Richard thought of all the possibilities but came up empty.

"How about a sense of humor?" Jesus asked. "You guys need to learn how to laugh."

Richard was struck by the obviousness of the question and wondered briefly why he hadn't been able to answer it himself.

"Think about this for a moment," Jesus continued. "What kind of world would you have if people were born laughing instead of screaming?"

As much as Richard thought about this question, he concluded that its implications were so mind-boggling as to render it unanswerable.

"You don't like that question, do you?" Jesus asked.

What do you mean?" Richard replied.

Jesus hesitated long enough to formulate what Richard should have already known.

"You guys don't like open-ended questions, do you?" he asked. "You like everything in a nice, neat little package—an answer for everything. The unknown scares the hell out of you, doesn't it? Forget about life's great questions. Those things don't matter, and not having a sense of humor is killing all of you. You know, anyone can die, but not everyone can live. You guys just need to get off your butts and get over yourselves."

Richard found himself bent over with his elbows on his knees and his head in his hands. Of course, Jesus was right.

A long silence went by as Richard, again, realized how truly fucked up the human race really is. Once more, he asked an obvious question.

"So, is it too late?" he asked.

"Too late?" Jesus replied. "It's never too late. You can find something funny in just about anything." "I guess that explains terrorism," Richard added. Jesus nodded slowly as his response came to the surface.

"I don't know about that," he said. "Maybe. Now personally, I think that a terrorist is what you get when conception happens in the rectal cavity. But that's just me."

They looked at each other squarely in the eyes and suddenly burst out laughing to the point of tears.

"That's hysterical!" Richard exclaimed.

"Yeah," Jesus began. "It took me a while to come up with that one."

A few minutes passed as their laughter subsided.

"So," Jesus continued. "I guess I've been doing a lot of the talking. Tell me a joke, Dick, and not the one about the aristocrats. That one's just nasty."

Richard searched himself for a joke that might be on par with Jesus's sense of humor without going over the top. He knew the joke Jesus was referring to and used it as the line between humorous and disgusting.

"Um, give me a minute," he began.

"Come on, Dick," Jesus said. "Don't let me down."

"Oh, I got one!" Richard interrupted. "Uh, what did Jeffrey Dahmer say to Lorena Bobbitt?"

Jesus paused to consider what the punchline might be.

"I don't know," he answered.

Richard delivered the punchline while holding back his laughter.

"So, uh, you gonna eat that?"

Jesus was unable to contain his laughter as the muscles in his face began to ache.

"Dude, that is sick!"

Even though Richard had told the joke many times in the past, he began laughing as well, demonstrating that laughter is, indeed, contagious. Again, they allowed their laughter to subside as the conversation took a serious turn.

"So, Dick," Jesus began. "You're a smart guy, a lawyer. You went to college. Tell me something, and be honest. What do you think of religion?"

Given the humor of their previous conversation, he found the question completely unexpected.
"I need to think about that one," he replied.
"Which one?"
"Does it matter?" Jesus asked.
"I suppose not," Richard answered.
When people talk about religion, it is assumed that the topic is regarding Western religion - usually, Christianity. Richard gave a deep sigh as he struggled for an educated opinion.
"Well," he began. "I think that the building of civilization is based on ideas. But its destruction is based on religion."
Jesus's face was suddenly overtaken by surprise.
"Whoa, dude," he said. "That is deep. Now tell me why."
Richard went on to explain that those who practice beliefs not based on the existence of God tend to be much more peaceful and enlightened than participants of Western religions.
"Alright," Jesus said. "Why do you think that is?"

Here was the million-dollar question. People seem to be naturally aggressive, paranoid, and hostile. We are prone to self-centeredness and a strong tendency toward superiority, as has been repeatedly demonstrated throughout our history.

    Perhaps, on an unconscious level, people of certain religious persuasions believe that God allies Himself with them, leaving them to also believe that this deified alliance upholds what they deem to be morally reprehensible. Thus, they adapt the teachings of their respective religions to their personal opinions, intolerance, and judgmentalism when, in fact, the principles of what they claim to follow demand just the opposite approach: that they give up their sense of self to become part of something greater. A force for absolute good without conditions, prejudices, or exceptions. After several long moments, Jesus summed up his response.
"Dick," he said. "I have never heard anyone answer that question like that. Most of the people who come here just throw up their hands and say, 'I don't know'. But you...you

hit it right on the head. So, what does it all come down to?"

Richard had the right idea. Certainly, he'd formulated the cause of that particular social illness, but like many of the world's problems, there was only one root cause. One common denominator.

"Um, well," he began. "We're not really good at listening."

"Yeah, okay," Jesus agreed. "Why is that?"

The need for order tends to transform the simplest ideas into complex problems, and Richard's reaction served as a clear illustration of the human tendency to overthink a simple question.

"Come on, Dick. You're so close."

Another moment passed as Richard searched himself for what he knew was right in front of him.

"We never listen," he whispered. "Because...because we think we know better."

"Dick," Jesus said. "I'm impressed. Do you know how many of you guys realize that? A few, but not nearly enough. So, I'm gonna give it to you straight. You guys don't know anything. Two-thirds of your world is starving, and you can't fix that. You just can't figure it out because you don't know everything you think you do. Yeah, you come up with some interesting things, all those gadgets you have. You put all your energy into all this crap because you don't know how to solve your problems - the ones that matter. What's holding you back is your ego. You guys think you are the best thing to come along since the discovery of anal warts, and that's why you don't listen. If you did, you'd learn more. You'd set aside what you want for what you need. Keep it simple, then you can fix your world. Think about it. You could end hunger. What a concept! But if you don't learn to listen—if you don't learn some humility, you will fail. Then, everyone loses."

    Some say that money is the root of all evil. But by itself, money has no value. The root of all evil is ego. It is what drives greed, corruption, and selfishness. While others are allowed to starve, suffer, and die, the chosen few bask in the glory of wealth, comfort, and a full stomach. Ego is both counterintuitive and counterproductive, standing as an obstacle to human survival, intellectualism, and creativity. In order to consider what is good for the world, one must be able to think outside the boundaries of ego. This is the first step. Jesus's words made a deep impression on him, and he sat consumed in thought, that the one thing people are best at is selfishness. "Cheer up, Dick," he said. "You know, there is an upside to all of this. When you're finally able to starve each other to death, you can still come here."

This grabbed Richard's attention, believing that Jesus might be suggesting that people would be better off dead than suffering. And while some people believe this is so, Richard was stunned to hear that idea spoken by the Son of God.

"What?" he said.

"Well," Jesus began. "Would you rather be dead and comfortable or alive and starving?" It was not a fair question, but a ruse. A set-up designed to prompt Richard into thinking beyond what he'd always believed, on some level, to be the coming death knell of the human world.

"There is one other thing you guys need if you're going to pull this off," Jesus continued. "You need faith."

"You mean, in God?" Richard asked.

Jesus was quick to answer.

"Whatever, dude," he said. "There's nothing wrong with having faith in God. But you can have faith in yourself, too. Now, Buddha - nice guy, by the way - said that peace comes from within and not from any outside source, and I'm good with that. If that's how you want to roll, then go for it. But you have to have faith in something - something positive, something that benefits others. Got it? Progress should go forward, not back."

Richard clearly understood the idea of faith but also knew that within the human world, faith, of any kind, was in short supply.

He decided to ask what he would shortly realize was a dumb question.

"So, if we keep going the way we are, are we talking about some kind of apocalypse?"

Jesus looked at him in disbelief.

"Seriously?" he giggled. "Dude, you've been reading too much of the Bible. Don't worry about all that stuff. The only apocalypse there's going to be is the one you're creating, and it's already started. So, there's not going to be boiling oceans and mountains on fire and the dead coming back to life. It's going to be something you're a lot more familiar with. All of that revelations stuff was probably written by someone hallucinating in the back of the cave."

A silent tension returned as Richard tried to imagine what the end might be.

"Hey, Dick," Jesus continued. "Forget about all that. Everything dies anyway."

Jesus noticed the expression of concern on Richard's face and redirected the conversation to his lighter subject.

"Hey Dick, what's your favorite band?" he asked. Again, Richard was pulled away from what was clearly a serious issue.

"What's my favorite what?" he asked.

Given the previous discussion regarding humankind's inevitable demise, Richard was taken aback by this sudden change in the conversation.

"Your favorite band, dude," Jesus answered. "Everyone's got a favorite band."

Richard gave the question a bit of thought. "I'm not much into music, to be honest," he answered.

Jesus was more than a little surprised.

"Not into music?" he said. "How can you not be into music? How can you consider yourself to be alive if you don't listen to music?"

His question left Richard without an answer.

"I guess I just don't have time."

Without missing a beat, Jesus offered a kind lecture on the necessity of music. It is something that, in some form, has been with us since humankind developed language and expression. It is part of who we are and intimately bound to our collective soul. Its rhythms, notes, and emotions possess a language that transcends the spoken word and lays to ruin our ideas of logic and intellectualism. A single note or chord can elevate one's consciousness, create a new paradigm, and change the minds and souls of those it touches. Its very existence is one of the things that makes us human and should never be set aside for lack of time. There is always time for music. His words left a deep impression on Richard as he, once again, sat lost in thought over one of the things that had been missing from his life. Jesus slapped him on the shoulder, breaking his stream of thought.

"Hey, guess what my favorite band is. Go ahead, guess."

The idea of the Son of God having a favorite band was something Richard found beyond unbelievable. Many types of music have been invented throughout human history, and making a 'guess' was impossible.

"Um, I have no idea," Richard replied.

Jesus brought out a bong. Its bowl already full of his own 'toasted honey'. He took a deep hit as he raised a hand, pausing the conversation and as its enlightening effect took hold, his face developed a golden glow.

"Where did you get that?" Richard asked.

"Hey," Jesus began. "Did you forget where you are? This is heaven, remember? You want something, you get it."

His surroundings were so earthly that, on occasion, Richard had to remind himself that he was indeed sitting on a park bench in heaven speaking with the Christian Messiah.

"Okay," he replied. "What's your favorite band?" "Pink Floyd, of course," Jesus answered.

It seemed ridiculous that Jesus would have a favorite band, much less a progressive rock band that began as part of the London psychedelic movement. Richard had quickly become caught up in a state of disbelief. "Seriously?" he said. "Pink Floyd?"

Jesus explained that what drew him to their music was not simply the lyrics, but the slow, drifting tones and wafting harmonies that seemed to slow the mind and cause one to slip into another place and time. "So, I guess you've got a favorite song too, huh?" Richard asked.

"Of course," Jesus replied. "Guess which one." Having listened to their music during his youth, he was more than familiar with them, but to pick out one song from their entire body of work was, again, impossible. "I have no idea," he replied.

Jesus dramatically stretched wide his arms. "The great gig in the sky, of course!"

Richard recognized the title immediately. "Of course," he said.

Jesus stood and, backing away by only a few steps, snapped his fingers as a microphone suddenly appeared in his hand.
"Check it out."
He turned around as music filled the air, soft and slow, led by an almost funerary piano. This was intertwined with the voice of an elderly man, summarizing the acceptance of his inevitable demise. With two strikes of the snare drum, Jesus began belting out the song's vocals like a rock star as a shaft of white light shone down upon him from the heavenly sky, spotlighting him as though on stage before millions. One could almost hear the deafening throngs chanting his name.
'Jesus!... Jesus!... Jesus...!'
As much as Richard enjoyed the song, there was one slight problem. Jesus was obviously tone-deaf and couldn't carry a tune in a bucket. A great song was growing painful with increasing intensity. With his hand over his ears, Richard noticed that everyone within a few yards also held their hands up, trying to block out what sounded like a screaming cat. Sensing the surrounding pain, Jesus stopped

and as the music faded, the shaft of light dwindled and vanished.

"Sorry!" he yelled. "Sorry, everyone!"

He turned and, walking back to the bench, tossed the microphone over his shoulder. It disappeared as it tumbled through the air.

"Wow," Jesus began. "My singing really sucks."

Richard responded with a slight degree of sarcasm as Jesus sat next to him.

"You think so?"

Jesus turned to him with a surprised expression. "Humor," he said. "I like it. There is hope for you." Sarcasm, it seems, can be aimed in one of two directions. As a vehicle of humor or as a weapon for hostility. Of course, if one is not receptive to humor, the expression of sarcasm can only end badly. Becoming more familiar with the target of one's jest is essential to realizing where humor is divided from cruelty. The difference is much like a flick of the ear, as opposed to taking aim with a rocket launcher. Jesus was embarrassed at his lack of musical skills and, again, offered an apology.

"Hey," he continued. "You know who's really good at this? Mary."
Richard replied with disbelief.
"The Virgin Mary?"
"Are you serious?" Jesus replied. "No, Mary Magdalene. Now she's got a great voice."
Richard remembered back when he attended Sunday school as a child.
"You mean the prostitute?" he asked.
"Well, she used to be," Jesus answered. "But she's here too."
This was no surprise to Richard, having learned that Jesus accepted everyone, regardless of the life they had lived. So, why not a prostitute? Why not a thousand? Obviously, anyone can join this club.

    As if on cue, a beautiful, dark-haired woman stepped out from thin air, materializing in front of them. She immediately captured the gaze of everyone around her as they admired her flawless beauty. Barefoot and dressed only in blue denim painter's pants, she walked gracefully to the park bench and sat next to Jesus. He had just finished rolling a joint, but before he could get to his lips, the slightly dark-skinned woman gently took it from his hand. She held it out and looked at Jesus expectantly.

"Oh, right," he said.

Doing the gentlemanly thing, he lit the joint as she took a deep hit. He turned to Richard.

"Always the lady," he said.

"Oh, sorry," he continued. "This is Mary Magdalene. Mary, this is Dick."

Richard nervously reached out a hand, and while she gazed into his eyes, merely nodded her head.

"She doesn't say much, but damn, can she sing," Jesus said.

By this time, Richard had become tongue-tied by her striking beauty, as she let a heavy waft of smoke trail into the air.

"Hey!" Jesus said.

There was a silent dialog moving between them as Mary's gaze held Richard in its grip. Jesus raised a hand to his shoulder and gave him a gentle shove.

"Hey, earth to Dick."

The sound of Jesus's voice got through just enough to break the catatonia induced by

Mary's beautiful, well-toned physique and smoldering brown eyes.

"What?" Richard replied.

"Glad to see you back," Jesus said.

He grinned as he cocked his head toward Mary.

"The boys never wrote about how hot she was, did they?"

Still, with a lost expression, Richard was forced to take a few moments to piece together even the most basic response.

"Um, yeah, I guess."

Just then, he was struck with something that was clearly missing.

"Hey, Jesus," he began. "Where are the disciples?"

Even though two thousand years had passed, Jesus remembered their faces with absolute clarity, and in Richard's mind, they should be in heaven as well.

"Well, you know," Jesus began. "Back in the day, we went everywhere together. I guess we just went our own way. You know, like the Beatles."

"So, they're not here?" Richard asked.

Jesus saw it necessary to again explain the

nature of heaven.

"You have to remember, Dick, what you see here is based on whatever your earthly reality was. All that means is that heaven is a really big place. Yeah, they're here, but what does 'here' mean? Now Judas, what a jerk. Turned my butt in. And for what—a few shiny coins? Yeah, totally worth it."

Richard grew somewhat concerned to see that the son of God might be holding a grudge. "Don't get me wrong," he continued. "He was just that kind of person, so it's all good. I guess I was just a little disappointed. I knew he was going to do it. I was just hoping he wouldn't. But what's done is done."

"So, where is he?" Richard asked.

Jesus paused to remember back to the day he was taken into custody.

"You know, I think he got a little lost." Richard looked at him with a quizzical expression. "What do you mean lost?" he asked.

"He lost his way," Jesus answered. "You can check out with your soul intact and come here, or you can be miserable and still end up

here with a clean soul. But if you're lost, you've got to find your way out first."
Given the course of his life, Richard understood what it meant to be lost.
"So," Richard began. "Am I staying here or am I going back?"
"Mmm, we'll get to that," Jesus answered. "Don't worry, Dick, we've got plenty of time."
Richard sat wondering about the choices he'd made during his earthly life. Now, he understood the consequences of making decisions, and he'd made more than a few, crediting his alcoholism as the result of his unwillingness to change.
"So, where are the marks?"
"Marks?" Jesus asked. "Oh, the marks." Jesus held out his hands, palms up.
"You mean from the nails? Seriously? Dude, that was two thousand years ago. Now, I don't know if you've ever been hammered up on a piece of wood before, but it really hurts. But I'm better now."
There was a slight lull in the conversation as Jesus remembered back to his earthly life.
"I suppose it could have been worse," he continued. "It could have been impalement,

but you can't rise from the dead with a pole sticking out of your butt, can you?"

Richard was somewhat familiar with that particular method of execution and, just for a moment, wondered which would be more painful.

"You know, both sound pretty unpleasant," he said.

"Yeah," Jesus replied. "But I think I'll take crucifixion anytime."

With Mary Magdalena still sitting next to him, Jesus reached a hand up and gently brushed the back of his fingers down the side of her face.

"Are you going to sing for us?" he asked.

Richard was suddenly struck by the feeling that the two might be closer than they appeared, and with that impression, his curiosity got the better of him.

"I don't mean to pry," he began. "But, are you two, uh...?"

Jesus turned to him and, with a slightly teasing voice, inquired about his question.

"Are we what?"

Richard felt embarrassed to even consider the question, much less ask it.

"Uh, you know. Never mind."
Jesus knew exactly what Richard was referring to and playfully continued his inquiry into Richard's nervous question.
"You mean, are we an item? You know, back in the day, it was a serious thing for anyone to marry a prostitute. I mean, you could get your butt kicked for that. It was a Jewish thing."
This brought the next topic of conversation to the surface.
"I have to ask you about something," Richards said. "We have this issue going on."
"Yeah," Jesus replied.
Richard hesitated, trying to find the right words for what he considered to be an uncomfortable subject.
"What do you think of gay people?"
There it was, out in the open. It was a topic that many found themselves too embarrassed or intolerant to talk about. However, Jesus certainly was not among them.
"Gay?" he said. "I don't think I've ever heard that word before. What does it mean?"
Had Richard considered this question more carefully, he would have avoided the conversation to begin with.

"Um, how do I explain this?" he began.
Jesus glanced at Mary as they both grinned slightly.
"Dick," Jesus said.
Richard was lost for words as he tried to think of a way to explain the meaning of the word as well as the behaviors associated with it.
"Dick, I know what you mean."
Richards' head snapped up as his attention was quickly broken.
"You do?" he asked.
No longer feeling the need to explain the idea of homosexuality to the Son of God, Richard let out a deep sigh of relief.
"Yeah," Jesus answered. "I was just messing with you. So why ask me?"
"Well," Richard said. "There's a lot of people where I'm from who protest against gay people, saying that God hates them. I was just wondering what you might have to say about it."
While Richard was speaking, Jesus reached back behind the bench and brought out a water pipe. Lighting the contents of the bowl, he inhaled deeply as his head glowed with the enlightening effects of what he earlier

referred to as 'toasted honey'. He briefly held his breath as a well-worded yet obvious answer came to him.

"Huh, gay people," he began. "Honestly, I don't care which way you roll as long as people love each other and don't hurt anyone. Other than that, who am I to stop people from being happy? Now, what do you think?"

Certainly, Jesus was not indifferent towards anyone, nor did he find sexuality sinful, and as Richard presented his views, they found themselves reaching the understanding that it is far easier to simply accept others without exception than to waste one's efforts and energies standing in angry judgment of those they were quick to condemn. There was a slight break in the conversation when Jesus turned back to Mary. She has also been smoking Jesus' particular brand of weed and has been fully enveloped by its effects. However, during her own experience of illumination, one of the straps of her painter's pants had inadvertently slipped down over her shoulder, exposing a tanned youthful breast. Richards' head fell

forward slightly as his mouth dropped open. He again found himself mesmerized by her statuesque beauty and although only one of her breasts had been exposed, Richard could not help but to see it in complete detail. It was flawless and held properly aloft by the perfect musculature of her upper body. Following where Richard's eyes had fallen, Jesus carefully reached out and pulled the strap back up over her shoulder.
"Come on now, Mary," Jesus began. "Dick's new here."
He turned back to Richard and spoke in a whisper.
"Sometimes, I think she does that on purpose."
Richard was still tuned out.
"Uh, okay," he replied.
Despite Jesus's gentle scolding, Mary continued with an obvious degree of suggestive eye contact. This did not go unnoticed, and Jesus saw fit to break the tension by, once more, requesting that Mary do them the honor of singing.
Reaching out towards Richard, she brought her joint to his lips, then gently caressed the

side of his face with the back of her fingers. He was so overcome by this brief experience that, had he been asked about it at a later time, he would be unable to recall it. She stood up and walked out to a place in the grass as the gray tones of the piano, again, could be heard building in the air. The voice of the elderly man, once again, came and went, followed by the double strike of percussion, cracking its way through the sky like twin lightning bolts, one after the next. At the first note that came pouring from her soul, a shaft of white light burst from the sky, striking her with the brilliance of an exploding star. It was the same song Jesus had attempted, but his rendition only served to demonstrate that feeling pain in heaven is possible, even for those who had been there for eons.

Mary's body quickly ignited into a white ethereal flame as her voice rushed forth like water from a burst dam. The eyes of every soul in paradise held her in their gaze while angels drifted down from their heavenly perches. Her voice, note for note, was a divinely inspired work of art, causing all who

heard it to fall into a profound state of ecstasy. Their eyes closed. Their heads tipped back while their bodies gave off a golden glow. Then, all at once, everyone drifted off the grass, hanging motionless on their backs. Initially, Richard fought the experience, struck by a sensation too odd for words. Jesus tapped him on the shoulder.
"Dick," he said. "Just go with it."
Richard gave in and soon found himself caught in a similar state; his mind sank into a blur as his soul rose to heights indescribable by any language. The music faded as its last notes drifted off into the ether. The ecstasy of every soul in heaven dissipated as Mary returned to the park bench. Turning to the side, she gracefully put an arm up along its edge and, reaching over, took the joint from Richards' lips and took a hit, inhaling deeply.
"There are just no words for some things," Jesus said. "Right, Dick?"
Richard was still engrossed in the sound of Mary's voice. He had never heard anything so beautiful and would likely never hear it again. Seeing this, Jesus decided to break the tension by bringing up a completely unrelated issue.

"So," he began. "What's with you guys and swearing?"
Richard was suddenly snapped back into the moment and inquired about Jesus's question.
"What?" he asked.
"Swearing," Jesus answered. "You guys really like to swear. Why?"
Richard paused to carefully choose his words.
"Well, I guess it helps us vent," he said.
"Alright," Jesus said. "But you do a lot of swearing at each other, don't you?"
Richard became noticeably uncomfortable, knowing that he had a strong tendency toward this behavior, especially in heavy traffic. He put a hand out towards Richard's shoulder.
"Dude, you don't have to be nervous about it. You swear a blue streak when you're driving, and I get it. It helps you vent your anger. What I have a problem with is when you start swearing at other people."
Richard was cautious in his response, realizing how important it was to be accountable for oneself. However, he felt as though he was being called out on something he was clearly guilty of.
"Um...yeah, I...um."

Jesus smiled slightly and gave him some much-needed reassurance.

"Dick, take it easy," he began. "It's not personal. I know you have flaws. You 'are' human, right?"

Richard was greatly relieved that he was being spared the embarrassment of a scolding.

"Now, there was Buddha, who once said," Jesus continued. "What was it?"

He took several moments to recall the exact words.

"Oh yeah. Being angry at someone is like taking poison and expecting them to die. Do you know what that means?"

Richard hesitated in his answer. As an attorney, his thinking was ruled by logic, and until now, deep spiritual thoughts had never been compatible with his personality. But with the changes he was experiencing, a different type of understanding was taking hold and with this new understanding, the answer became crystal clear.

"Um, that means that when we get angry, it only hurts ourselves."

Jesus was pleasantly surprised.

"Dick!" he began. "You're finally getting it! Now, we're getting somewhere."
Hearing this, Richard reached what was obviously a logical conclusion.
"So I guess we should stop swearing, huh?"
"I never said that," Jesus replied. "Honestly, I think there's a place for it. Now, as for myself, I don't roll that way, you know? 'Cause I'm Jesus. You guys just have to remove yourselves from all that anger. Do whatever you need to do to chill out. Try some meditation. Maybe take an anger management class. I mean, you guys do way worse than a little swearing, and really, they're just words. They don't hurt anyone. It's your anger that leads to conflict, and that's when people get hurt. But there is one word that really bugs me, and it's not even a swear word. It's a four-letter word that's been responsible for millions of deaths."
Richard was stumped. He always equated swearing with not only venting but hostility and violence.
"Give up?" he asked.
A moment passed as Jesus pointed at him and, with his thumb also extended up, said.

"It's the word 'fire'."

Richard was struck dumb. He had never before considered that any word could be used for the purpose of killing. But every language possessed at least one word used for the same purpose. Jesus knew that killing was not dependent on the use of any language. He was simply trying to make a point.

"I don't know if there's anything we can do about that," Richards said.

No longer pointing at him, Jesus allowed Richard to absorb the point he was trying to make until he finally stated what should have been obvious.

"And that's why you need to change," he said. "You can do it. It's as easy as throwing up, and you've been changing for millions of years. You do it all the time, but you still resist it. I mean, I'm the son of God and I can't figure that one out."

"I know we need to change," Richard replied. "I just don't know how we're going to do that. Hey, wait a minute. Did you say millions of years?"

A faint smile came over Jesus's face. He knew this topic would come up eventually.

"Oh, yeah," he replied. "That whole creation business. You guys take it so literally, don't you?"
He turned to Mary, who was still enjoying the transcendent effects of Jesus's personal stash. "See? What did I tell you? They still believe it's true."
Richard was lost. He'd spent a few years going to church as a child and knew the creation story as well as anyone else. And like anyone else, he was told time and time again that the universe was not born but created, but molded by the hands of God. Mary smiled and shrugged her shoulders.
"Dick, really?" Jesus continued. "Look, back in the day, I was a Rabbi. I taught this stuff all the time, so take my word for it; it's just a story, okay? All those people who call themselves Christians...they don't understand any of that, and the Jews spend their lives studying those first five books. You want to know what those things mean? Ask one of them."
A moment went by as Richard realized that the son of God was 'not' a creationist.

"Hey Dick," Jesus continued. "You don't really believe that story, do you? I mean, you've got an education, right?"

"Well," Richard began. "I guess I never thought about it until now."

Jesus searched himself for a simple way to help Richard understand the meaning beneath the words.

"Okay, do you believe that art mimics life?"

Richard had heard this saying before and had some degree of understanding for its meaning.

"Yes," he answered. "I'm pretty sure I know what it means."

"Alright," Jesus replied. "Let's look at the universe like it's a great masterpiece. Now, it took Michelangelo four years to paint the Sistine Chapel. What does that say?"

Richard spoke hesitantly.

"I guess all great things take time."

Jesus smiled broadly.

"That's right," he replied. "So can the universe be thought of as a work of art?"

Richard was quick in his response.

"Yeah, of course."

"Okay, so if anything beautiful takes time to create, then why wouldn't that idea apply to

the universe? Besides, there's something else in that book most people miss, mostly because it conflicts with the creation story. You want to know what it is?"
"Yeah, I'm curious," Richard answered.
"Okay," Jesus began. "It's been a while, so give me a minute."
He'd spent so much of his earthly life teaching from the Torah that its entire contents had become committed to memory.
"Oh yeah," he continued. "To God, a day is like a hundred thousand years, and a hundred thousand is like a day. So, if God exists outside of time, where do these six days come from?"
Richard's mind had suddenly become aroused by the need to understand more, but at this point, there was one important idea that had not occurred to him. We do not learn by answering the easy questions. We learn by asking the difficult questions.
"So, the creation story really is just a story?" Jesus nodded with a grin.
"Dick," he began. "As a collection of books, the Bible is well-intentioned, but it's only as rational as the person reading it. Why do you

think there are so many religious lunatics out there?"

Richard agreed without hesitation, as the conversation took a very different turn.

"I know this sounds like a stupid question," he began.

"But what's Satan like?"

"Satan?" Jesus replied. "I always thought that name was a bit dramatic. I just call him Fred."

Richard was surprised that such a notorious character would be known by such a harmless name.

"Trust me," Jesus continued. "He's not what you think he is."

Richard was puzzled by this response. But just as he was about to inquire further, he was startled by a voice coming from behind him.

"Hey, J.C!" it began. "How's it hanging?"

Jesus rolled his eyes in frustration as two figures stepped out of thin air.

A man and woman, both dressed strangely, walked up behind Richard. One might use the word clownish as an apt description. Despite his frustration, Jesus took the time for a proper introduction.

"Dick, this is Fred. Fred, Dick."
He stepped up to Richard with a broad toothy smile and quickly grabbing his hand, shook it aggressively.
"Dick," he began. "How's it going?"
Still clasping Richard's hand, he turned to Jesus.
"I can see where the nickname comes from." It seemed that one of Fred's strongest traits was his ability to be rude, and making eye contact with Richard completed his insult. "Nothing personal, Dick, but you do have that look."
Richard tried not to let himself be annoyed, in spite of Fred's attempt to harass him. But seeing that Richard was unaffected by his malicious jab, Fred released his hand and stepped back.
"Eh, it was worth a shot," he began. "Don't worry, Dick. I can do a lot better than that."
Again, he displayed a wide smile that gave him the appearance of someone who would pat you on the back with one hand and stab you with the other. Fred introduced the woman he arrived with as his wife, Lilith. She was tall, shapely, and wore straight, jet-black

hair. Her complexion was a snowy white, offset by fire engine red lipstick. Her body was clad in tight black leather that exposed every contour of her physique. Every curve and cranny made itself visible. Out of sheer curiosity, Richard quickly scanned her from head to toe. But this did not go unnoticed, and as Richard's eyes swept over her, she raised her left leg and, bringing her foot to the bench, exposed the shape of her most delicate place. This prompted Richard to sweat profusely as his face flushed a deep red. Lilith reacted with a faint grin of satisfaction.
"So, Dick," Fred began. "What do you think? Pretty hot, isn't she?"
Richard noticed Fred's personality as being somewhat juvenile and had difficulty believing that he was the keeper of the underworld. He seemed more like a college frat boy, living to party, waking the next morning in a puddle of his own vomit, but going back for more the following night. Lilith, however, seemed to be all business. The way she stood indicated a great deal of strength, but her expression hinted at an obvious streak of cruelty. Clearly, she was the

one who wore the pants in the family. Now, Fred turned to Jesus with a teasing voice.

"So," he began. "How's the son of God today?"

Jesus was already growing tired of him.

"Come on, Fred," he replied. "Remember whose house you're in."

Richard was suddenly struck by the question of why the devil would be allowed in heaven when his place was clearly with the damned. He leaned over towards Jesus and whispered, "What's he doing here?"

Upon hearing him, Fred spoke up immediately.

"Well, Dick," he began. "We have this arrangement. I get to show up once in a while, but only if the big guy here thinks it's important. So for some reason, I'm supposed to be here."

Richard surmised that every issue has, at least, two sides, and if Jesus was giving his opinion, then perhaps the devil should get equal time.

"So," Fred continued. "What are we talking about?"

Jesus was patient with his answer.

"We're talking about people."

"People?" Fred replied. "Please, don't even get me started. I mean, I thought I was evil, and I am, but I'm not capable of some of the things you guys do. Makes me a little jealous, really."

It was at this point that Fred noticed Mary. It wasn't often he was allowed into heaven, but he knew Mary on sight and, purely out of his arrogance, began aggressively flirting with her.

"Hey Mary," he said. "Lookin' hot as always, I see."

It seemed, for a moment, he'd forgotten that his wife was standing nearby, and her response was an immediate slap across the head. Fred raised his hands in a protective manner.

"So," Jesus began. "I see you two are still getting along."

Mary took another hit from her joint, and as the two women made eye contact, a heavy tension developed. Jesus was the first to notice.

"Alright, ladies," he began. "You know the rules. None of that stuff here."

The tension eased as Lilith fixed an angry glare at Fred, and as he rubbed the back of his stinging head, Richard decided it was time to take a verbal jab at him.
"So," he began. "I guess you're used to this, right?"
Fred paused as he looked at Richard.
"Oh, that was nice. Hey, we should hang out sometime. Seriously, if you want to take a vacation someplace warm, come on down."
Richard felt a bit put off by Fred's impromptu invitation and looked to Jesus for advice on how to respond. Leaning toward him, Jesus spoke in a quiet voice.
"Probably not a good idea."
For the benefit of setting aside Richard's discomfort, Jesus quickly changed the subject. "Anyway," he began. "Me and Dick have been talking about religion, and I thought you might want to pitch in."
Fred was not known by Jesus as being especially bright, but after a few moments of thought, found something to contribute.
"Religion...mmm. I suppose there is nothing wrong with it, and as long as people are killing each other over it, then I'm good with

it. I mean, when people think they have the big guy on their side, they're going to think they're on the winning team, right? So, I say, let them do it. It's not like you can change the way they think."

Everyone fell silent as the conversation took an unusual direction. It seems that Fred, allegedly lord of the underworld, was in favor of religion as long as its participants were acting out of hate and personal judgment. And although his point was valid, it was his approach that Richard questioned.

"Coming from you, I guess I shouldn't be surprised," he said.

Fred threw up his arms defensively.

"Hey, I'm just doing my job," he said. "But you know who I like? Conservative Christians. Or, as I like to call them, religiopaths. Now, those guys are my kind of people. I mean, they really know how to hate."

Hearing Fred's remark, Richard decided to take the issue a step further.

"So you think they should be allowed to kill each other?" Richard asked.

Fred looked at him with a quizzical expression.

"What do you mean by each other? Don't you watch the news? They don't kill each other, they're too busy killing everyone else. If it was television, that would be my favorite show. It could be called 'Killing for Peace'. Awesome. They could turn it into a game show."

Jesus looked at him impatiently.

"Hey Fred," he said. "Shut up."

Richard was taken aback by this almost hostile exchange and turned to Jesus with a wide-eyed expression.

"He really tests my tolerance sometimes," Jesus whispered.

Fred put an arm on Lilith's shoulder and began giggling as she turned towards him and growled slightly. Both Richard and Jesus expressed a somewhat fearful look as Jesus quietly voiced a warning.

"Here it comes."

Lilith slapped Fred's arm from her shoulder as he continued chuckling in amusement.

"Hey, watch this," he said. "Hey Lilith, go make me a sandwich."

His remark was met with a swift reply as Lilith brought up a fist and struck him across the face, hard enough to send him to the ground.
"Ow, what the fuck woman!?" he shrieked. Immediately, the small girl who had greeted Richard upon his arrival appeared between his knees, and before Fred could get to his feet, the child raised a foot and stomped on his testicles.
"No swearing!" she yelled.
Fred howled in pain as Lilith grinned broadly.
"Shit!" he bellowed.
This was, again, met with the firm impact of the little girl's shoe as she ground Fred's testicles underfoot. Richard turned to Jesus with a curious question.
"Why did you let him come here?" he asked.
In his reply, Jesus decided that a little humor was in order.
"Well," he began. "I knew he'd get himself into trouble. I guess I just needed a good laugh."
Finally, Fred was able to get to his feet and, with his hands out in a guarded manner, made his way over to the bench. He walked,

hunched over, and sat next to Richard while cupping his still-painful testicles. His temper flared as those around him snickered at his expense.
"It's not funny!" he yelled.
"Fred," Jesus began. "You never learn. Every time you've been here, you do the same thing. And every time, the same thing happens, and you wonder why people laugh at you."
By this time, Fred was near tears as the pain between his legs began to mount.
"Anytime, Fred," Jesus said.
Richard looked somewhat confused as Fred continued roaring in pain.
"Come on, Fred. You know how this works."
"Alright!" Fred yelled. "Just make it stop!"
Jesus had already decided on removing his pain but paused for a few moments as he sighed in resignation.
"Okay," he said.
Jesus made a backhanded gesture towards Fred as the pain left his previously aching testicles.
"Now, what do we say, Fred?" he asked.

Although the pain was gone, Fred was still weakened by its intensity. Too weak to be stubborn.

"Thanks, JC," he said.

He was still gasping for breath when Richard interrupted.

"Um, I don't mean to change the subject, but I'm staying here, right? I mean, you said we'd talk about that."

Jesus nodded briefly.

"Yeah, I did say that, didn't I?"

He took a moment to construct his response, knowing exactly where the conversation was going.

"I don't know," he said.

It was certainly a response, but far from an answer. Richard became both bewildered and frustrated over an answer he had not expected.

"Wait," he began. "I thought you knew these things."

Jesus heard these things said often and always answered the same way.

"I don't have a clue," he continued. "Really, it's up to you. You're the one who decides."

Richard continued in his frustration.

"But you're Jesus!" he began. "I thought that when someone died, it was because you..."
"Dick," Jesus interrupted. "Dick, relax. Take a breath, okay?"
Jesus asked Mary for her joint and, handing it to Richard, spoke in a reassuring tone.
"Just chill out for a minute."
Richard took a deep hit as Jesus looked at Mary with concern. Fred took the opportunity to speak on Richard's behalf.
"You know, JC," he began. "He does have a point."
Jesus looked at him with a frustrated expression.
"Fred, shut up."
Fred threw up his hands and took a step back.
"Alright," he replied. "I'm just sayin'."
Turning back to Richard, Jesus resumed the conversation.
"So, you want to know if you're staying. Let me ask you this. Do you have the will to live?"
His question caught Richard off guard and was at a loss for an answer.
"Yeah, I guess," replied.

"You guess?" Jesus asked. "Dick, we can talk about anything you want. You want to ask questions? That's fine. Some questions don't have answers; you know that. But this is something you have to be sure of. Now, do you have the will to live?"

Richard was not fully aware of the gravity of the question being put to him and answered after a few moments of thought.

"Yes," he said. "Absolutely."

But in considering the seriousness of the issue, Richard had failed to see the consequences of his response.

"I'm glad to hear that," Jesus replied. "Because that means you're going back."

"What?" Richard asked.

He felt as though he'd been tricked and looked back at Fred, thinking he would supply a second opinion.

"Hey, don't look at me," he said. "I have no say in these things."

Richard was confused and afraid. Knowing what led to his arrival in heaven, he was terrified of what was waiting for him once he returned to his earthly existence.

"Well, what if I don't want to go back?" he asked.

Jesus spoke reassuringly.

"Dick, look, you made up your mind already. I can't choose these things for you. Think about it; it could be worse. You could be going with Fred."

Richard turned to see Fred looking at him with a broad, toothy smile.

"Yeah," he said. "You're right. So, what now?"

Even before the moment of his arrival, Jesus had something special in mind for him. He knew the outcome of his accident would likely change his life forever, but Jesus also knew that he could make use of Richard's experience and that change can sometimes start with one person.

"Okay," Jesus began. "Here's what I want you to do. Talk to people. Tell them what I've told you because they're not listening to me anymore."

"Why me?" Richard asked. "No one's going to listen to me."

Jesus grinned slightly.

"Dick, you've got to trust me on this one, okay?"

"Hang on a second," Fred interrupted. "Don't I get a crack at him? Shouldn't he get the chance to show how much he stinks?"

His tone was a bit playful, but underneath the humor, Fred's request was quite serious. He believed that Richard deserved the chance to prove himself worthy of heaven, but also believed that he should have an equal chance to achieve eternal damnation.

"Come on, JC, fair is fair."

"Fred, shut up," Jesus replied. "You're not getting this one. He has a job to do."

Like anyone else, Richard's greatest fear was the unknown. He had arrived at a place he could never have imagined and was about to return to a world he was far more familiar with. He had an idea for the seriousness of his injuries. Yet, the unknown was in the nature of his recovery. It would be so much easier if his body were allowed to die, leaving him to continue his ethereal existence by Jesus's side. But he realized that anything worth doing should be difficult, and the same could be said for life in general.

"So, how much will I remember?" Richard asked.

Jesus raised a hand as a blurry circular patch of space dissolved behind him, leaving a brilliant white field in its place.

"Everything," Jesus answered.

Richard closed his eyes and held his breath as he prepared to be sent back to his earthly life.

"Okay, do it," he said.

He cracked an eye open to see Jesus raising a glowing hand.

"Oh, wait," Jesus said. "I've got something for you."

Richard opened his eyes out of curiosity and found Jesus holding a hand out, a glowing white ball hovering over his open palm.

"This is for you. Consider it a gift."

Richard gazed at it in wonder as Fred began pacing in frustration, knowing that he would not be allowed to pursue him for his own sinister intentions.

"Shit!" he began. "I never get anything!"

It was only moments before the small girl appeared once again, running up to him in a blur. But being struck with an idea, Jesus waved her off.

"Hang on a second," he said.

The small girl stopped and, putting her hands on her hips, looked at him with an irritated expression.

"Just wait."

He turned to Lilith for a favor.

"Lilith, can you shut him up?"

She grinned and, nodding her answer, walked up to Fred, who was still ranting. He stopped ranting as his mood quickly changed.

"Hey baby," he began. "What's up?"

Lilith stepped in close and grabbed him aggressively by the front of his pants.

"You want to do this here?" he asked.

No sooner had he completed his question than Lilith pulled him in and thrust her knee up into his groin. The pain left him unable to speak as he crumbled to the ground. The little girl giggled in amusement as Lilith walked back to the bench to see Jesus nodding his approval.

"So, where were we?" he said. "Oh yes, this is for you. You'll figure it out later."

Before Richard could get out a single word, Jesus, still with the opaque orb drifting above his hand, gave him a quick slap across the

side of his head. The ball of light caused Richard to glow as he looked at Jesus in confusion, as though expecting an explanation. Sometimes, explanations are necessary, making things easier to understand. Other times, explanations only serve to circumvent the work involved in learning and enlightenment. As Richard was overcome by the light that had enveloped him, Jesus grinned slightly and waved.
"Be seein' ya' Dick."
Making a backhanded gesture sent Richard off the bench and hurtling through the bright patch of light that hung in the air. Growing dimmer, it vanished moments after Richard disappeared from view. Having witnessed Richard's departure, Fred got to his feet and, hobbling over to the bench, sat with his hands still cupping his testicles. After this last assault, he decided it was better to be calm and well-behaved. But out of curiosity, he turned to Jesus and inquired about what he'd seen.
"Alright, what did you do?"
Jesus lit another joint and, handing it to Mary, gave an evasive answer.

"I just gave him a little something."
With the pain subsiding, Fred sat up and asked Jesus for a joint. His request was met with a giggle from both Jesus and Mary.
"You're joking, right?" Jesus answered.
"Yeah, that's all I need—an enlightened Satan. What could possibly go wrong?"
Before Fred could ask again, Jesus changed the subject and asked Lilith for her impression of Richard. Her answer was brief, to the point she raised a foot back onto the bench.
"I really wanted to fuck him."
The small girl who had terrorized Fred with her repeated attacks on his groin reappeared, only to be frightened off by a deep, intimidating growl from Lilith. But, as she darted away in a blur, Jesus turned to Lilith with a punitive remark.
"God, Lilith, you are such a bitch."

Chapter 3

His eyes opened slowly, and as Richard's head began to clear, he discovered his hands had been tied to the rails of a hospital bed. As he attempted to raise his head, he felt the resistance of hardware that had been fixed to his skull. Richard wasn't exactly sure about where he was, but he did realize that he was in a hospital as the sounds of IV pumps and other machinery filled his still foggy mind. A nurse walked into the room carrying a plastic graduated container. She began to kneel next to the catheter bag that hung from the bed frame when she noticed his eyes blinking. Putting the container on a nearby stainless steel table, the nurse quickly walked up to Richard's shoulder.
"Richard," she said.
Blinking again, he made eye contact, and seeing this, the nurse took it as a positive indicator of awareness.

"Richard, my name's Tabitha. You're in the hospital. You're in intensive care at Maine Medical Center in Portland."

She raised an index finger in front of Richard's face and asked him to follow it with his eyes. The nurse was quite pleased to find that he could follow commands, and stepping out, she returned with the resident in charge of this case. The doctor put two fingers into Richard's hand and asked him to squeeze. He was only partly successful in that, during the accident, the pothole he struck shattered the bones in his shoulder, ripping tendons and muscles from their anchor points. The doctor pulled a wheel-mounted computer over and reviewed Richard's X-rays and CT images. Two bones in his neck had fractured against each other, yet his spinal cord remained intact. The doctor was not an especially religious man, but he was struck by the impression that, given Richard's injuries, the fact that he was even alive was nothing short of a miracle. He returned to Richard's bedside and, assuming he could understand him, updated him on his condition.

"Richard," he said. "You were in a car accident; you hurt your neck and your shoulder, but it looks like everything's going to be okay."

As the doctor walked out, he was met by Richard's wife, who was also updated on his condition, and as soon as the conversation ended, she walked into the room as the nurse was emptying the catheter bag. Stepping up to the head of the bed, she took his hand and quietly spoke to him.

"You had us worried for a while."

Richard looked into her eyes and uttered a short response.

"How long?"

His wife hesitated as she looked at the nurse with an expression of concern. As much as she wanted to give him an answer, she also wanted him to stay calm.

"He needs to be oriented," the nurse said. "You can tell him, just keep it short."

She turned back to him and calmly told him that it had been a week and a half since the accident that had nearly taken his life. He also had two separate surgeries. One to repair his neck and the other to reassemble his shoulder.

Three days later, Richard was transferred to the orthopedic unit on Maine Medical Center's sixth floor. From there, he continued to recover as bits and pieces of the accident returned to him. But there was something else, something that seemed foreign, coming to him in flashes like a ghost darting across the room. Initially, Richard concluded that this was the result of the hydrocodone being given to him intravenously. But as the dose was reduced, the flashes turned into small fragments, wafting up from his memory. Eventually, they would coalesce into his waking mind, and as promised, he would remember everything.

Richard was healing quickly. Even by the normal rate of the body's ability to mend itself, his doctors were at a loss to explain how such severe injuries could recover so quickly, and two weeks later, Richard was transferred by ambulance to Portland's New England Rehabilitation Center. Another two weeks went by as he regained nearly complete movement and functioning. Another series of X-rays were taken, showing nothing more than the plates and screws in his neck, as well as the metal staples in his skin. One week into his stay, the staples were removed, leaving the incisions to heal on their own. By this time, the circular hardware that had been keeping his neck immobile had been removed, and he was allowed to walk, needing little assistance.

Two days before his discharge, Richard woke to a strange odor. It smelled familiar, yet he could not recall from where. Bringing his hands up to his face, he checked to be certain it wasn't something he'd touched, but upon examining his fingertips, he discovered an odd yellowish stain on his index finger and thumb. Unable to rub it off, he walked to the bathroom and filling his hands with water and liquid soap began washing them thoroughly. Yet, the stains remained. He rang his nurse for a few alcohol pads, but this too proved ineffective. Returning to his bed, he again brought his fingertips to his nose. This time, the smell disappeared, but out of curiosity, he touched his skin to the tip of his tongue. Immediately, he noticed the slight taste of honey. But, there was something else, something that brought all the pieces together - the momentary impressions, the fleeting fragments of memory. Everything came to the surface as his mind was pulled into another place where he recognized the park he'd visited, the faces of those he'd spoken with -- even the image of the little girl who raced her way around heaven, chastising violators of proper language. Every word that had been spoken cascaded into his conscious mind. For Richard, this recollection was nothing short of life-altering, and sitting on the edge of his hospital bed, he began to quietly weep. Now, he understood and somewhere within him, a door had opened leading down a path few are willing to take.

    He would do exactly as he had been asked, to convey his experience to anyone who would listen, and there would be many drawn simply out of curiosity. But there was one more thing he would, in time, discover. The gift he had been given would soon make its way to the surface.

Chapter 4

Days turned to weeks as Richard continued his recovery, and, upon returning to his doctor for several follow-up visits, it was noted that he was still healing at an astonishing rate. He had stopped drinking and, at some point, decided to leave the law firm, thus the stress it had created. Recording his experience on paper, Richard was persistent in bringing it to the eyes of as many people as possible. Soon, it was in print and selling in the millions of copies. Taking his small family with him, he set out every summer for several years on a lecture circuit. Some attended out of curiosity, while others for spiritual reasons. But no matter where he went, when he encountered people up close, he noticed how their moods would suddenly change. Bickering turned to laughter. Arguments ended in cooperation, and indifference transformed itself into kindness. Richard continued with his life as a man without a religion. He saw it as restrictive and an obstacle to a productive, peaceful spirituality where the only required practice is kindness. He spoke as he believed, that with this single practice, all the elements of change would fall into place. The lectures he gave as well as the book he'd written were designed to convey this point: that in order to have a better world, we must become better people, led by the necessity to change. He had also begun referring to himself as Dick.